PARASITE KINGDOM

ALSO BY BRAD RICHARD:

Habitations
Motion Studies
Butcher's Sugar

Parasite Kingdom

POEMS

Brad Richard

THE WORD WORKS
WASHINGTON, D.C.

Parasite Kingdom © 2019 Brad Richard

Reproduction of any part of this book in any form or by any means, electronic or mechanical, except when quoted in part for the purpose of review, must be with permission in writing from the publisher. Address inquiries to:

The Word Works
P.O. Box 42164
Washington, D.C. 20015
editor@wordworksbooks.org

Cover art: Kelly Anne Mueller
Cover design: Susan Pearce
Author photograph: Famous Genius

LCCN: 2019930522
ISBN: 978-1-944585-28-0

Acknowledgments

I am grateful to the editors of the journals in which some of these poems have previously appeared:

Connotation Press: "The Little Girl Who Lives in the Palace Square," "Firewood Gathering"
Green Mountains Review: "Homecoming"
New Orleans Review: "Love Song"
Poets for Living Waters: "A Cento of the Garbage Patch"
Sakura Review: "How the Torturers Come to Truth"
Witness: "Fear"

Some of these poems were also published in the limited edition chapbook *Larval Songs* (Antenna, 2018), a collaboration with artist Kelly Anne Mueller.

"Making It Great Again" appeared in the anthology *If You Can Hear This: Poems in Protest of an American Inauguration*, ed. Bryan Borland and Seth Pennington (Sibling Rivalry Press, 2017).

for Tim

Contents

What Lay Under Joy: Explicating the "Tunnel-Bundle" . . . 11

I Describe; I Explain . . . 15

I.

The Wasp Knows . . . 19
Fear . . . 20
The Cry . . . 22
Firewood Gathering . . . 23
The Little Girl Who Lives in the Palace Square . . . 24
Finding the Fathers . . . 25
Four Photographs of a Man Carrying a Child . . . 26
How the Torturers Come to Truth . . . 28
In the Interrogation Room . . . 30
Surveillance Notes . . . 32
Asylum . . . 34

II.

Waspocrypha . . . 47

III.

Making It Great Again . . . 59
A Cento of the Garbage Patch . . . 60
Love Song . . . 63
War Story . . . 66
You Have No Idea How Bad It Was . . . 68
Mirror . . . 70
Toilet Paper . . . 71
Ecophobia . . . 73
The Baker . . . 74
The Palace Astronomer Explicates the New Sky . . . 75

IV.

Larval Psalm ... 79
Testament of the Blue Wasp ... 80
The King in His Chambers, Dying, Alone ... 82
Winged Fictory ... 83
Palace Inventory ... 84
Burrow Inventory ... 86
How I Will Remember Paradise ... 87
After the Last War ... 89
Economy ... 90
Homecoming ... 91

Notes ... 97

Thanks ... 99

About the Author / About the Artist ... 101
About The Word Works ... 102
Other Word Works Books ... 103

It is not down in any map; true places never are.

—Moby-Dick

What Lay Under Joy:
Explicating the "Tunnel-Bundle"

It was a time of monsters: military police and other state actors who tortured their prisoners, including children; scientists who conspired to feed the delusions of a tyrant; that tyrant, a king trapped in his own paranoia, either powerless to control the widening chaos—civil war, foreign threats, rapid environmental collapse—or indifferent to it. Others were beasts spawned from the imago of a gigantic blue female wasp, the king's nemesis, who lived in a burrow beneath the palace. Real or imaginary, she had a cult; her followers died for her, and the deaths of their enemies were often ascribed to her supernatural intervention.

I recall the discovery of the "tunnel-bundle," as the popular press has named it. (Scholars refer to it by the name printed on the cloth in which these documents were bound: Parasite Kingdom.[1]) This occurred during the site excavation for the Temple of Secular Joy in our global capitol, when a worker swung his pickaxe, heard and felt his blow's impact reverberate beneath him, and then, when the patch of earth where he stood collapsed, fell into what turned out to be an ancient tunnel complex. Despite extensive forensic research, the bundle was the only artifact found. No trace of the builders of the tunnel complex, and no clue in its blank, curved walls as to its intended purpose. A royal tomb? A secure location for a besieged government? A hidden sanctuary for the rites of a forgotten cult? A mine? Its convolutions have been meticulously mapped, but no entrance or exit has been found. Its shape has been interpreted by archeologists, symbologists, conspiracy theorists, and religious fanatics, but no theory thus far proposed adequately accounts for it. Indeed, most scholars agree that rather than

---

[1] I must here acknowledge Dr. S. Bernofsky, who singlehandedly translated the bundle's contents and, in the process, gave the fullest possible account of its language, which she named Symbiontish. Although some have felt that such a darkly-purposed tongue should remain extinct, Dr. Bernofsky is at work on the libretto of a Symbiontish opera, *The Wasp and the Whale*, set to premiere on the theatrical cruise ship *Radney Steelkilt* two years from now.

being a key to mysteries of a lost civilization, it is without plan or purpose. Other than the bundle, it is the most complete artifact we have of the madness of its creators.

On the evidence of the bundle, that madness was not confined to the palace and its inhabitants. Some citizens—apparently, those trapped by the worst of the fighting in the neighborhoods closest to the palace—were reduced to brutal lives. Their suffering made them prone to morbid beliefs and delusions, coping mechanisms that allowed them to survive (if, in fact, they did survive). Others, who lived far enough way from the fighting to live relatively normal lives, were at the least psychologically affected. Some of these were inspired to become what I classify as "citizen-prophets," whose eccentric, hermetic visions they (or someone else) took the trouble to transcribe. For the most part, such people could live as if their world were not ending, and, unlike their less fortunate fellow citizens, they could still operate for a time within the framework of their basic comforts. And yet the horror, never so distant as they may have believed, permeated their psyches and weaponized their comforts.

Where was all of this happening? And when? What nations were involved? And why did they all behave as madly as their maddest citizens? Is any of what is described a depiction of historical events? If these are fictions, what inspired them? I have spent seventeen years on these and other questions raised by the documents collected here. We all, of course, grew up on a folk history of a bellicose, exploitative, self-destructive, technologically and morally limited culture that supposedly preceded ours, although the archeological record provides no evidence. As entertaining and instructive as those stories may be, it is hard for a rational person to conceive of the tribalism, greed, and sheer cruelty that motivates those characters. We may accept them as psychological archetypes, but imagining them as real people committing real acts strains credulity. Yet the "tunnel-bundle" exists. Does it provide our only concrete evidence that this nightmare realm was no myth but an actual civilization (if that word can even be applied)?

As a scholar, I am troubled. The inconsistencies in this very incomplete record are immense: there are multiple narrators, some of whom may or may not be the same[2]; the wasp changes size at will; the war is over, and then not. The intended order of the texts is not clear. Some show evidence of editorial annotation—by whom, we do not know; others, particularly the "Waspocrypha," display so much manipulation and distortion that, without further discoveries that shed light on its sources, we may barely apprehend the text and its meanings. (Who, for instance, were Ahab, Jonah, and Hamlet? What was capitalism? Where was Paradise? What was that apparently majestic creature, mentioned but once, in a simile, the whale?)

But those are scholarly concerns, relatively minor. What disturbs me most, what horrifies me as a human being, after having devoted the long twilight of my career to these texts, is not merely the possibility that what they describe is, in fact, historically true; it is that such evil may yet lie dormant within us, like a larva waiting to awake and burrow out of us into lethal flight. I have sometimes even believed that the Parasite Kingdom has never gone away: that we are its inheritors, and that we will meet some inevitable version of its fate.

I fear the words of the ancient philosopher: "Truth can never be told so as to be understood, and be believ'd."

>   Dr. E.A. Melville
>   Prof. Emeritus, Ancient History and Culture
>   Greater Global University

---

[2] I have also imagined that both possibilities are true: that there is one narrator who is also infinitely many; this leads to the intolerable possibility of an infinite multitude of kings and kingdoms and wasps, a fractal system of horrors extending through all time. And I have imagined myself as that narrator.

I Describe; I Explain

Fleeing the slaughter, I hid in the museum,
where snipers' laser sights
wouldn't find me. Found a service door

blown off its hinges. Emergency lights.
Registrars' offices.
Dim galleries. The Grand Hall: smashed vitrines,

pummelled statuary. Dolls I'd loved as a child lay gutted,
their royal faces smeared
with feces by soldiers, rebels. From the rubble, I took hold

of a granite hand's rough grip. As if it knew me.
Bullets spurting—I sprinted
the limestone stairs to the unfinished

Rotunda of the Blessèd Martyrs. Tracer-lit,
blast-seared, holy portraits
glowered from niches. The Wet Nurse, The Teacher,

The Priest, straining to catch The Angel
of Agony's gaze. Breast
and belly scaled, blue-black like her veined wings.

Her eyes starless night, its sheen reflecting me.
Boots and shouts rushed the stairs—
Too late, Narrator, cried the Angel. *Start over.*

I

The Wasp Knows

Hooked in sockets between her eyes, her antennae rise. Scape, pedicel, bristly flagella: muscles make them flick and pivot as she tests the air, tuning in—scents, hints, who's her sister, who's her worker, who's her babies' dinner, where's that cordite blowing in from, where not to be when that just-launched missile lands. How many of her nests have they blown up by now? They've driven her to ground while their drones fly free.

Her antennae measure what's left of her terrain: Is this cell big enough for a grub to grow? Is this burrow family-sized, or a snug bunker for solitude? A quick sweep of burrow walls tells her *hard earth cool as river mud, hard work of my ancestress, scraping out this haven for queens*. It's quiet here, beneath the palace. Pressed to the ceiling, the tips of her flagella pick up the faint rumble of trucks, tanks, boots playing chase overhead.

But he's no child, her enemy. If she blocks out the burrow's stale breath and ticking heart, antennae pick up voices twitching, ants caught in the shifting grit packed between burrow and palace. She tracks the voices back, climbs the circuitry inside the palace walls, rides electromagnetic waves pulsing syllables to the king's ear, feels them tap his eardrum and vibrate his ossicles, phonemes exciting pheromones as he gibbers into his phone, finger now swiping its screen, coaxing images begetting images—a raindrop swollen with light, a rose, a kitten, a child with baby goats, a fast car, cars racing, limos like black beetles crowding the entrance of a gold hotel, a flag flying from an aircraft carrier, oil-slicked birds, bombers dropping bombs on hillside villages, cratered hillsides, rubble-clogged streets and streams, a child's cratered eye . . .

She feels what a wasp feels, lets her antennae rest, but checks in often on the palace, learning the true dimensions of her burrow, his kingdom. Listening, she slips in signals of her own, pricks to let him know she's there, ready to end his long war.

Fear

One morning Fear was a little kingdom
inhabited by flags and burnt matchsticks

and me, scuttling down cratered avenues
to the library, where my job was making sense

of what was left of the world. Our king
sulked in a dim corner, pretending

to read old magazines, eluding for now the grip
on his shoulder, the usurping voice: *time's up,*

your highness, the librarian will put those away.
I bowed; he nodded. His thin lips made me think

of the one-armed girl eating dirt in the square.
The day was hot, the building stank; decades

of pigeons roosting and dying in the attic
had tainted stacks of diaries, histories, novels,

atlases and lexicons of extinct empires, I
their final guardian, our king the relic and oracle

of uncatalogued silences suffered and stored.
Dust shook down, windows rattled as tanks groaned

in the street. Open-mouthed, staring like a boy scout
stripped of his badges, the king let me lead him

to a basement table and give him my pocket knife
and a carton of unreckoned contents of his regime.

As I dragged more cartons from the shadows,
he slit open files and envelopes, studied photographs

of people with amputated names, transcribed tapes
of a woman whispering in a closet, scraped samples

from crumbling confessions, scanned columns
of numbers and burned them and sniffed their smoke,

nodded in a trance, his gaze so rapt I bent
my ear close to his lips, hoping for a hint—

A shell burst above us, a shadow whimpered
behind me: he cowered as boots pounded down the stairs,

and I was glad to snatch my knife away, glad to point
to his dank little uniform, glad to let them open

the ledger of my body, to feel their bayonets
inscribe me with their cleansing lies.

The Cry

We hear shrill bone piercing metal,
throat severed from its pledge.

We hear the cry, feel it shape the silence
of our bodies, a silence without wings.

Rubble mutes the boulevards.
Bomb plumes smother the horizon.

Rubber soles clamber up the stairs,
squeal on linoleum: children, home

from scavenging, find us in the dark.
They brush dust from our faces.

What was that noise?
Nothing; just a bird.

What was it singing?
The song of its fathers.

Our fathers?
The song of our fathers

would split a bird's heart
and crush its skull like a nut.

Oh! Teach us that song!

Firewood Gathering

When soldiers fire tracers over the old school you can see what's left   maybe you'll get lucky and make it to the thicket by the swamp   if they haven't already stripped it for themselves then you'll just have to pull small timber from the rubble nothing too big to carry don't drag anything   that's how they tracked your father

That gas the palace guards set off in the market   can you taste it in this tea   and it still burns my eyes   I wish I didn't have to send you out tonight   but you're brave aren't you a brave girl and don't you want a hot meal tomorrow   make a basket with your skirt like this   you'll be surprised how much it can hold

Of course you'll have to go back to the market tomorrow   pay the boy for these potatoes and tell him I'm sorry   we don't want him to think we're thieves   I think I went to school with his mother   or her sister   anyway he has her face didn't you think he had pretty eyes   maybe you'll go to school with him one day

Don't be afraid if I'm not home when you get back   my eyes hurt so bad is there water in the bucket   if your aunt could walk me to the river   I know she's dead   anyway I can make it on my own   anyway you know how to break up the wood and sort it   it's fun if you use the little song I taught you

> *baby's fingers mother's fingers father's fingers king's*
> *this boy's arm and that girl's leg rifle barrel rib*

You probably won't come home with anything   you'll have to find something else to sing   come down to the river   help me wash my eyes

The Little Girl Who Lives in the Palace Square

The sentries fix their sights on her back
        just for practice
as she wanders the square,
        rolling a dark ball between her palms.

From the tower they track her shawl,
        and the radio plays anthems,
and the girl sifts rubble
        for cool stones to suck.

And the girl remembers sirens, the bomber's whine,
        a nights-long spasm,
        an oilfield burning,
she remembers her mother's hands.

She remembers her mother's hands
        bright against the sky, against walls
collapsing, her mother's fists
        exploding, burning against brickwork.

Stop now: time to gather
more specks of dung, bits of paper,
        clumps of sand
from the firing squad wall.

She rolls them with her spit into the ball,
        staining her hands
        with all the kingdom she owns,
but mouth's so dry stone sticks to her tongue.

The sentries fix their sights on her back.
        Cool as sky, her mother's hands
cinch her shawl and tuck her in the shadow
        of the palace flags.

Finding the Fathers

In the library, in the meat lockers,
in the terminal's unclaimed luggage,

in the shadow of the palace, in the ruins
of the veterans' hall and the hall of justice,

in the pill bottle, the confessional,
in the jailhouse showers and the peephole

of the interrogation room door,
in unmarked boxes and specimen jars,

in shoes, trousers, belt, shirt,
in scar, birthmark, bruise, orifice,

in muzzle, cylinder, spent cartridge,
in urn and reliquary, cipher and glyph,

in letters to our mothers, letters
from the general, the warden, the king,

in photograph and footage, in charred
teeth and scattered ash, in rhymes

we used to sing when we played
we used to sing when we played.

Four Photographs of a Man Carrying a Child

1.
White haze eating away these buildings
White dust of these buildings suspended after a barrel bomb blast
Rubbled cinderblock warped corrugated sheet metal scraps cartons
        pipes rags where the street was
Slow hurry of haze toward the man running with that big child in his arms
The man's head wrapped with a scarf or shirt the child's too and his face
The child's left arm dangling disjointed right arm half-raised as if trying
        to help to lift somehow his weight a little to lessen it for the man
Balanced mid-stride on left foot right leg raised so his thigh hoists
        the child's weight back up onto his arms
Keeping them for now upright

2.
Background a crowd making of themselves an ambulance because
        there is none to carry the body they must move
Two others rush toward them as the man and child run away
Urgent the orange stripe down his jacket's front orange plackets
        on his pockets orange cuffs
Purple the child's sweater red the blood smeared on his face from
        which he stares
Dead ahead *I am no dead boy*

3.
A brick wall standing should hold a child in a room
This man pulled this child from walls' rubble
Hair blood-matted left arm hooked around the man's neck
Behind them a young man's gesture says *careful where you step*
Where is there to go

4.
Slender tree no leaves no color trunk snapped near the base
A car its insides burning doors pocked from the fire or are those
        bullet holes
The child's face powdered with ash his arms locked around the
        man's neck
The man almost sprinting in his orange-striped jacket
He doesn't look at the car doesn't look at the camera
It's like he's looking inside himself for a whole clean place to take them
Black smoke towering from where the car's roof was

How the Torturers Come to Truth

On the wall the sergeant writes a word
you've never heard before we tell its story:
"'We come to *truth* as you first learn a sentence.'
Can you explain the meaning of this passage?"
The word sinks through you, leaves a hole
to bury not the meaning but the body.

We come to truth the way you learn your body
has been defined by lawful hands and words.
We thread our wires deeper into your holes
to teach you what your role is in our story.
You'll learn no cipher guarantees safe passage
when you are not the author of your sentence.

We come to truth as fragments of a sentence
because the mutterings of Nobody
echoed all night along the passage
after the slow dissection of your word.
Across the land the ending of your story
crawls back to fall more bloody in its hole.

We come to truth. We look into the hole:
hair, teeth, excrement. We make a sentence
to hold what isn't there: Inside the story,
someone's pulled a sheet across your body,
now muddled in the shadows like a word
erased in the dark, fouling the passage

where you'll come to truth, this sealed-off passage
that serves as well as any other hole.
If someone asks about you, there's no word.
The desert spreads before us like a sentence
erased by morning, no trace of the body
that might insist on telling its own story.

Truth comes, of course, telling its crazy story,
of which it cannot verify one passage.
Like a bullet as it leaves the body,
without memory of blood, bone, or hole,
we hear the judge pronouncing one more sentence
against our enemy, your word.

Listen: our story is all that keeps us whole.
Every bent passage, each bruised sentence
breaks our bodies on the truth of the word.

In the Interrogation Room

I think you've mistaken me for this son
you think I have, the one you imagine

I might have seen riding some mule cart
down the alley toward the palace last night

when I was taking out the trash. True,
I *was* taking out the trash, a chore I might've given

my son, had I a son, as you've imagined,
but no, just me carrying kitchen scraps

wrapped in that morning's paper, the one
with the king's birthday letter, *Dear Children,*

you are the best gift I could ask for, same
as last year, same picture, same smile stuffed

in the bin in the alley. Past curfew? Yes,
but the trash stank, no, it *really* stank,

like those trenches along Palace Square
we're not supposed to talk about. No,

no one else was out, certainly no cart
loaded, as you describe, with explosives,

of which I, being a priest, am ignorant. Yes,
I heard the explosion. Yes, I went inside. Yes,

you're right, it *is* odd about my vestments
having gone missing, but I haven't worn them

for so many years now, perhaps my late wife
stored them or even sold them after the ban

on the temples, which, I know, we're not
supposed to talk about, but here we are.

Had I a son, your suspicions would be reasonable,
and had I a son who did this, I would turn him in,

but my wife and I were childless. You're sure
the cart that blew up by the palace was driven

by a priest? Hard to believe. Yes, I'd love
a cigarette. God save the king. A son

would be a blessing in these times.

Surveillance Notes

The clock tower strikes a foreign midnight.
Shivering, we analyze the chill, then the feed
from the eye we planted in the kitchen ceiling
of our subject, escaped poet (**P**). She's answering
an asylum questionnaire with the timely help
of a native "neighbor," wired lady in our pay.
What (**P**) struggles to describe, our receiver
translates as hiss, buzz, and our lens reads
(**P**)'s lamplight so brightly hot, pages flame out,
blank in our viewer—fragile devices, like us,
hidden in homes or plain on a park bench, watching
one lit window as if it were the moon. Faces
emerge if you look long enough . . .

Mountains, my god, we crossed for this . . .

Question: Do they have the same questions for (**P**)
on their side of the mountains as we do on ours?
Behind darkened glass, we watched her spit and bite,
resisting truth we offered as current surged through her.
With their questionnaires, their dictionaries, their smiles,
would we have answers? Could we bring her back . . . ?

Noted: their task finished, (**P**) and her neighbor laugh.
They're pouring drinks, smoking cigarettes.
The neighbor shows (**P**) something beautiful
on her phone, free hand tracing bodies in air,
or contours of a map? or letters of insect alphabets?
Slowly we become accustomed to seeing without
understanding. We raise our spread hands, block out
the moon. Noted: no light squeaks through. We fold
our shadows with our faces and tuck them
in pouches for later . . .

The neighbor's gone, leaving (**P**) at the window
looking at the moon? the clock tower? her eyes
in the windowpane, floating over the river?
She moves, the window darkens. We'll know
what to say to forgive ourselves after,
our subject, our verb, our object;
homeward now . . .
                              Noted:
we're in her head with a clear feed.
She thinks she's free. She thinks
she's got a good shot at a new life,
that maybe they'll understand her here.
Sweet darkness without paths.
It'll look like suicide. It was.

Asylum

This morning, dozing on a bench by the fountain,

I dreamed of crossing a gorge
on narrow planks of light

when something blunt nudged my shoulder:
a cop's baton. He smiled, watched me walk,

waved and wouldn't stop until I waved back.
                            I went to the library,

took out my application—
What other names have you used

(include maiden names and aliases)?
Do you fear harm or mistreatment

if you return to your home country?
Are you afraid of being subjected to torture

in your home country or any other country
to which you may be returned?

Left it blank. I wanted to read—

no books in my language, so I searched
the Geographical Encyclopedia until I found

the kingdom I escaped: *ringed by mountains . . .*
unstable military dynasty . . . wasp-infested . . .

When the librarian woke me, at first
I thought I was home.

Asylum: all my language offers me
is *burrow* or *cell*. My caseworker said,

"Be patient. Given where you come from
and what you claim, we're not entirely sure

you exist." I laughed; she didn't. She gives me
notebooks, cigarettes, canned meat, tells me

not to tell. No clutter on her desk: phone,
a few folders, pens, photographs. She has

a husband, a daughter. I asked, "If I'd arrived
with children, would this be easier?"

She stared, tapped her pen. "You say you're a poet.
Imagine cages for your imaginary children."

[reconstruction—original damaged in transit][1]

My mother believed in the Wasp,
[...] wasp charms around my neck,
taught me wasp rhymes, wasp games,
made up bedtime stories for me

[...] the Dormant Queen. "Pray, [she'll protect *] you."
When soldiers stormed the attic and found our guns,
Mother slit her throat on the stairs.
[...] [dark blood gleamed *] [...] the steps.

---

[1] Brackets with ellipses, [...], indicate gaps in text due to damage in transit during wartime. Text in brackets with an asterisk, [*], is a best guess where readings of the original are uncertain (illegible, smeared, stained, etc.). —Editor.

The park, packed with noisy families,

strolling groups of old soldiers. A child runs up
to a stooped vet in dress uniform, snaps her heels,

salutes. Grinning, the old man rewards her
with a white paper aster from his pocket.
                                            The cop

from yesterday walks up to a black man
on a bench, stares until the man leaves; sees me,

smiles and hands me a flower
as I hurry out to the street.
                        The wire stem,
coiled at the flowerhead's base.

Library's closed—some local holiday.

They've moved me from the detention center
to this apartment building. "No one knows

your language there," said the customs officer.
"You'll be safer. We'll keep an eye on you."

I keep thinking of the woman, her nipples
leaking milk through her shirt, crying

in the common room. No one talked to her.

Tonight I stayed in with a book
my caseworker loaned me, by the poet

every child here learns by heart.
I sounded out lines. They dried my mouth.

[reconstructed fragment—original damaged in transit]

[...] fingers like [...]
[...] her perfume and the [screams *]
and [...]

[poem—found intact]

Dear interrogator, doing laundry tonight
in a detention center basement, I thought of us
in that laundry room of yours, bare box springs
propped on chairs, extensions cords stripped
to bare wires, a washer churning in the corner,

Dear interrogator, as I fold these shirts,
still warm, I remember not so much
your questions as tepid water doused
over bound me on box springs,
not so much answers as hot
surges from wires through flesh,

Dear interrogator, here's your answer,
this shirt, my favorite, stippled
with bloodstains, perfect match
for the scars on my back, one worn
over the other, I connect the dots

Can't sleep. Climb to the rooftop,
watch boats on the river.

Lean against the ledge, hands shoved
deep in my coat pockets, feel

antennae? legs? Aster petals, crumpled
in my palm, detached from their stem.

                              (Kid next door still crying.
                              Soldiers took his mother.)

I've washed my empty meat cans

and stacked them on the counter,
dozens, one for each day

since my application was filed.
That wet meat smell.

That *what, me?* smell.

Caseworker called: "Today."

She tapped her pen on her desk
while two gray-suited investigators

laid out their analysis
of my poems and statement.

My description of the interrogation room?
"Obviously a hospital." The torture

my body proved? "Such resistance to therapy
to treat a psychic rupture—occasioned,

perhaps, by grief—is not uncommon,
even here. Surely you agree

your best help waits at home."
        "Good luck,"

she said, holding out her hand.
I let the suits lead me away.

[reconstruction—original damaged in transit]

One day, the King visited our [...]
Our teachers lined us up along [...]
backs to the wall, an arm's length apart:

no touching, no talking. I stood [...]
by the exit door that went [...]
    The King arrived: a coat cluttered [...]

topped with a general's hat, like a [...]
on a mannequin, with no face I [...]
His words sounded taped. Had I heard [...]

    Lately, when I read aloud [...]
I've written, the words sound [...]
    Have I said this [...]

This time the planks of light
span blank space. If I stop

moving I'll fall, but the light
holds me as it narrows, sharp

inside me—
          The train stops,

lurches me awake. Two soldiers
escort me off, lead me to the trailhead

at the mountain's foot. Months now
since I hiked down to here. Frost

on withered weeds and brush.
High up the trail stand two royal guards,

rifles across their chests.

I start to climb. "Wait,"
one of the soldiers calls. "Tell us

what it's really like there,
on the other side." Past the guards,

the trail disappears. Gray rocks,
gray sky.

        There is no other side

II

Waspocrypha

(Supplied by a Late Assistant File Clerk of the Imperial Archives)

[That anxious clerk—wary in thought, glance, word, and act: I see him, always dusting his sealed cartons and locked cabinets with a queer handkerchief, embroidered with a kind of Möbius labyrinth whose stitched paths burrowed to what seemed to be but never was the reverse side of the cloth. He dusted his archives like a sentry scanning his post, watching me at my table, alert for every enemy, within, without—or like a rebel hiding in the ranks, awaiting a signal meant for him alone.

I handed him my requests; he laid out books, photocopies, microfiches, files that opened with a whiff of cordite. He helped me navigate websites only he could find—"For this, we pirate the palace wi-fi," he snickered. I hear him still, whispering as he leaned over me at my table in that airless basement, telling me his versions of the archive's contents as if they were his confessions, his gospel, his secrets.]

And God created great wasps.
    Genesis.

> In the free element above me flew,
> Fluttered and dived, in play, in chace, in battle,
> Insects of every colour, form, and kind;
> Which Photoshop® can't paint, and aeronaut
> Had never seen; from dread Vespidae
> To honeybees that buzzed from flow'r to flow'r:
> Gather'd in clouds immense, like flying islands,
> Led by mysterious instincts through that lush
> And fecund region, though on every side
> Assaulted by voracious enemies,
> Kings, CEOs, and soldiers, arm'd against wing'd life,
> With crop-dusters, napalm, and phosphorus bombs.
>   *Montgomery's World before Capitalism.*

I do not know whether, when a new and different order of things has succeeded after the destruction of the world . . . it is not wonderful that at the present time a snake should be formed out of a dead man, growing, as the multitude affirm, out of the marrow of the back, and that a bee should spring from an ox, and a wasp from a horse, and a beetle from an ass, and, generally, worms from the most of bodies.
  Origen, Contra Celsum, 248 CE.

Now the Lord had prepared a great wasp to burrow into Jonah.
  Jonah.

Out of his nasoþurles dropped wormes out like wasps.
  Mirk's Festial, ca. 1450.

In the year 100 before the birth of Christ, as Julius witnesseth it, an infinite multitude of wasps flew into the market of Capua and sate in the temple of Mars. They were with great diligence gotten out and burned solemnly. Yet they did foreshow the coming of the enemy and the burning of the city.
  Histories, Topsell, 1658.

There go the drones; there is that Wasp whom thou hast made to fight therein.
  Psalms.

If we compare sea animals in respect to magnitude, with those that take up their abode in deep burrows, we shall find they will appear contemptible in the comparison. The wasp is doubtless the largest animal in creation.
  Goldsmith, Nat. Hist.

If you should write a fable for little flies, you would make them speak like great wasps.
    Goldsmith to Johnson.

If a wasp stings you, your foes will get the advantage of you.
    a proverb

The great Wasp that maketh the sands to seethe like boiling oil.
    Lord Bacon's Version of the Psalms.

Immense as wasps, the motion of whose vast wings can in a peaceful calm trouble the sky till it boil.
    Sir William Davenant. Preface to Gondibert.

> That solitary beast of air
> The Vespid, which God of all his works
> Created hugest that burrow in the earth.
>   *Paradise Lost.*

> ——There the Vespid,
> Hugest of living creatures, in the earth
> Hunched like a fetus sleeps or broods,
> And seems a prisoner; yet her antennae
> Draw in, and in her mind revolves the world.
>   *Ibid.*

Scarcely had we proceeded two days over the desert, when about sunrise a great many Wasps and other monsters of the sand, appeared. Among the former, one was of a most monstrous size.... This came towards us, open-mouthed, raising the dunes on all sides, and beating the sand before her into a foam.
    Tooke's Lucian. "The True History."

And what thing soever besides cometh within the chaos of this monster's (wasp's) thoughts, be it beast, fighter jet, or bomb, down it goes all incontinently that foul great burrow of hers, and perisheth in the bottomless prison of her mind.
    Holland's Plutarch's Morals.

We saw also abundance of large wasps, there being more in those southern skies, as I may say, by a hundred to one; than we have to the northward of us.
    Captain Cowley's Voyage round the Globe, A.D. 1729.

Venus . . . the "wasp star."
    Star Gods of the Maya: Astronomy in Art, Folklore, and Calendars, Susan Milbrath, 1999.

Allah has assigned the fig wasp (blastophaga) to help pollinate the fig flowers.
    Dr. Zaghloul El-Naggar, 2017.

A wasp flying into the house is a good omen.
    a proverb

If a wasp builds its nest in your house, it is a sign that you will not live there long.
    a proverb

The Male Wasps are lesser than the Queens.
    Derham's Phil. Trans., vol. XXXIII, 1724.

To increase the size and potential of the penis: Take shuka hairs—the shuka is an insect [wasp] that lives in trees—mix with oil and rub on the penis for ten nights… When a swelling appears, sleep face downwards on a wooden bed, letting one's sex hang through a hole.
    Kama Sutra, Vātsyāyana, ca 400 BCE-200 CE.

[T]he ovipositor [is] a complex device found only in females. In many species of Parasitica, the mechanism serves both as an egg-depositing tube and a sting, allowing a female wasp to temporarily paralyze a host so that an egg can be laid upon or within it.
Solitary Wasps, Kevin M. O'Neill, 2001.

The ovipositor of a wasp is larger in the bore than the main pipe of the water-works at London Bridge, and the water roaring in its passage through that pipe is inferior in impetus and velocity to the eggs gushing from the wasp's ovaries.
Paley's Theology.

Ten or fifteen gallons of venom are thrown out of the stinger at a stroke, with immense velocity.
John Hunter's account of the dissection of a wasp.
(A small-sized one.)

This wasp's brain was two cartloads.
Stowe's Annals.

The papers were brought in, and we saw in the Berlin Gazette that wasps had been introduced on the stage there.
Eckermann's Conversations with Goethe.

PETRUCHIO
Come, come, you wasp; I' faith, you are too angry.
KATHARINA
If I be waspish, best beware my sting.
PETRUCHIO
My remedy is then, to pluck it out.
KATHARINA
Ay, if the fool could find it where it lies.
PETRUCHIO
Who knows not where a wasp does wear his sting? In his tail.

KATHARINA
In his tongue.
PETRUCHIO
Whose tongue?
KATHARINA
Yours, if you talk of tales. And so farewell.
PETRUCHIO
What, with my tongue in your tail?
> *The Taming of the Shrew, Act. 2, Sc. 1*

The wasp stung him in the abdomen, and her larvae probably hatched there in a moment.
> *"The Wasp and Her Would-Be Captors, or A Soldier's Misadventures and the Wasp's Biography, Gathered on a Homeward March."*

Myself have agreed to try whether I can master and kill this Burrow-Queen wasp, for I could never hear of any of that sort that was killed by any man, such is her fierceness and swiftness.
> *Richard Strafford's Letter from the Bermudas. Phil. Trans. A.D.1668.*

> Which to secure, no skill of leach's art
> Mote him availle, but to returne againe
> To his wound's worker, that with lowly dart,
> Dinting his breast, had bred his restless paine,
> Like as the wounded whale to shore flies thro' the maine.
> *The Faerie Queen.*

Being once pursued by a wasp which he had wounded, he parried the assault for some time with grenades; but the furious monster at length rushed on the tank; himself and comrades yielding to her ovipositor when they saw the onset was inevitable.
> *Missionary Journal of Tyerman and Bennett.*

God is not like a Waspe, which when she hath stung cannot sting again.
    H. Smith, Sermons, 1591.

By art is created that great Wasp, called a Commonwealth or State—(in Latin, Civitas) which is but an artificial queen.
    Opening sentence of Hobbes's Wasp.

The sovereignest thing on earth is venom for an inward bruise.
    King Henry.

Several wasps have come in upon this coast (Fife) Anno 1652, one eighty feet in length of the burrow-queen kind came in, which (as I was informed), besides a vast quantity of venom, did afford 500 weight of eggs. The wings of it hang for an awning in the garden of Pitferren.
    Sibbald's Fife and Kinross.

A tenth branch of the king's ordinary revenue, said to be grounded on the consideration of his guarding and protecting the cities from mercenaries and robbers, is the right to royal wasps, which are blue queens. And these, when either shot from the air or caught near the border, are the property of the king.
    Blackstone.

Sometimes the wasp shakes its tremendous wings in the air, which, cracking like whips, resounds to the distance of three or four miles.
    Scoresby.

Revolution—a great wasp stinging the hindparts of tyrants.
    Edmund Burke. (somewhere.)

In that day, the Wasp with her sore, and great, and strong sting, shall punish Leviathan the polluting serpent, even Leviathan that crooked serpent; and she shall slay the king that hides in the palace.
    Isaiah.

> "Soon to the sport of death the crews repair:
> The Queen unerring o'er their heads suspends
> Her sleek sting, and every turn attends."
>   *Falconer's Shipwreck.*

In their way they saw many wasps sporting in the barracks, and in wantonness filling up the soldiers with their venom and eggs, which nature has placed in their stingers.
    Sir T. Herbert's Voyages into Asia and Africa. Harris Coll.

It is impossible to meet a wasp's larval host lying on the road without being struck by his near appearance. The swollen belly seethes, with yellow seepage from the pores, and the eyes, paralyzed open from the venom's action, have a totally different air from those engaged in regular combat.
    Warfare and Wasps.

Suddenly a mighty mass emerged from the sand, and shot up perpendicularly into the air. It was the wasp.
    Miriam Coffin or the Wasp Hunter.

> Bright shone the roofs, the domes, the spires,
> And rockets blew self driven,
> To loose their momentary fire
> Against the vault of heaven.
>
> So fire with larvae to compare,
> The soldier serves below,
> Envenomed by a wasp in air,
> To express unwieldy woe.
>   *Cowper, on the Queen's Invasion of London.*

> A sniper perched on a ledge one night,
> The wind so thick it choked;
> Now bright, now dimmed, were the bombed rooftops,
> And the phosphor gleamed in the wake of the Wasp,
> As she burrowed through the smoke.
> *Elizabeth Oakes Smith.*

… and the breath of the wasp is frequently attended with such an insupportable smell, as to bring on a disorder of the brain.
Ulloa's South America.

suggestions sometimes flash through the mind which startle us as the poisoned sting of a wasp
Abraham Kuyper, The Work of the Holy Spirit, 1888.

Very like a wasp.
Hamlet.

A wasp seated herself upon the head of a snake and, striking him unceasingly with his stings, wounded him to death. The snake, being in great torment and not knowing how to rid himself of his enemy, saw a wagon heavily laden with wood, and went and purposely placed his head under the wheels, saying, "At least my enemy and I shall perish together."
Aesop

TAMORA
Let not this wasp outlive, us both to sting.
Titus Andronicus, Act 2, Sc. 3

> So be cheery, my lads, let your hearts never stop,
> While the bold harpooneer is striking the wasp!
> *Nantucket Song.*

> Oh, the rare old Wasp, mid storm and fight
> In her earthly lair will lie,
> A giant in might, where might is right,
> And Queen of the boundless sky.
> *Wasp Song.*

> Wasps in the sky
> God's voice deny.
> *T. I. Primer.*

> It is lucky to kill the first wasp of the season.
> *a proverb*

[*He could tell I was no scholar, didn't bother helping me keep track of sources, just put things before me and took them away, tucking them back safely in his nest of paper and dust. I don't vouch for the accuracy or veracity of any of this, and merely offer it as an artifact of days and nights spent underground, where we both sought refuge from the battles above, until one side or other might claim us, or until, like the prophet Ahab, we might say, "I am madness maddened."*]

III

Making It Great Again

Yesterday was *amazing*. The sky bled,
so we took a picture, added cloud-bandages,
and captioned it "me saving the sky ☺."
The lilies of the vacant lot were choking
on their own vomit, so we took a picture:
"I ♥ lilies ☹." It felt good to be doing something.
It felt good to be saying we felt something.
Then our lamps and streetlights, our phones
and laptops started choking on their vomit,
and darkness slimed. Through the goo, we watched
video of the good old days—not ours, I guess,
but still, nice to see nice people smiling
over a man who fell black on his head, and police
whitely walking a girl to school while crowds cheered.
Today, we'd have to shoot her. Did I say that?
Sorry, I meant we love one another so much.
Too much, maybe. Gives me a headache. My head
hurts, where is it? Who has it? Who stole it
and dropped it in this septic tank in this
unclean bed where it saw things and tasted
all the uncleanness all your uncleanness
it was you it was you it was you—

Tomorrow's gonna be *amazing*. Wait and see.

A Cento of the Garbage Patch
dedicated to Captain Charles Moore

nurdle: a plas
tic pellet; raw material of   production, or ground down
from larger chunks of   ;

                                          waterborne   mermaid tears

Much have I traveled in the
plastic stew

It is not down on any map;
true places never are
       twice five miles of nurdle ground
       twice the size of Texas
              a slow, deep, clockwise-swirling
              vortex of air and water

                                      turning
                                      turning
                              in the widening
                   North Pacific subtropical gyre

Japan   San Francisco

Now   from all parts the swelling landfills flow
          and bear their nurdles with them
          sweepings from cities and ships   junk nets ropes
          bottles motor-oil jugs cracked bath toys
          drowned turtles plastic stinking sprats plastic
          dead birds and ketchup-caps come tumbling down
                                                     the flood

you cannot stand in the middle of this
like stout Cortez when with seagull eyes
he stared at the Pacific—

        the sea
        a collector, quick to return
        a rapacious look
                        Look there, look there

        Oh my Atlantic of the cracked shores
        Are you—   —too?

25 percent of our planet   a toilet that never flushes

            hungor inan slat   merewerges mod

And so it piled up to the ceiling
it filled the   , it   the floor
it cracked the   blocked the door
at last the garbage reached so
      final   touch   sky

We borrowed a wheelbarrow
glazed with rain water

        But then, of course, it was too late

            What, no life?
        nurdle   nurdle
          nurdle   nurdle
              nurdle

                                             shored against my ruin

            the magnanimity of the sea
                        which will permit no records

[Sources, often altered, mingled, nurdled: Wikipedia, "nurdle" entry; "On First Looking into Chapman's Homer," John Keats; "Our Oceans Are Turning into Plastic . . . Are We?," Susan Casey, www.bestofonline.com; *Moby-Dick*, Herman Melville; "Kubla Khan," Samuel Taylor Coleridge; "The Second Coming," William Butler Yeats; "A Description of a City Shower," Jonathan Swift; "A Grave," Marianne Moore; "Crossing the Atlantic," Anne Sexton; "I'm Nobody! Who are you?" Emily Dickinson; "The Seafarer," Anonymous; "Sarah Cynthia Sylvia Stout," Shel Silverstein; "The Red Wheelbarrow," William Carlos Williams; *King Lear*, William Shakespeare; "The Waste Land," T.S. Eliot.]

Love Song

Forgive me. I thought I was dead,
your flag draped over my face,

dolls across my lap. I want to leave.
I want to thrash out from under

the swelling crest of the dollar
before its undertow swallows us

like a snack. *I'm going to eat your heart
like a snack.* You're going to eat my heart

before this undertow swallows us.
Swollen crest of the dollar,

I want to thrash out from under
the dolls across our laps. I want to leave

no flag draped over our faces.
(*Forgive me*, I thought. I was dead.)

✦   ✦   ✦

Thank you. I'm finished. If you care,
then rinse the soot from my mouth.

Here's a dollar. Let me know
if the future left a message

I can swallow. The newscaster
tells me the story of our lives

before I can check the ballot.
Before I can check, the ballot

tells me the story of our lives.
I can swallow the newscaster.

If the future left a message,
here's a dollar. Let me know,

then rinse the soot. From my mouth,
thank you. I'm finished, if you care.

✦   ✦   ✦

Forgive me. How little it took
to legislate assent, the way gods

make themselves appear natural.
I love the way you masturbate.

You make a ring of nudes in a meadow
feel lonely. The long night comes

when you have no one left to talk to.
When you have no one left to talk to,

the long night comes. Feel lonely?
You made a ring of nudes in a meadow

yours. I love the way you masturbate,
make them selves appear. Natural

to legislate assent this way: "God,
forgive me!" How little it took.

✦   ✦   ✦

Forbidden, we wipe ourselves away.
What difference does it make?

Like any liar, you know the trick.
"Fuck you." Just aim.

It only leads to more fire.
If beyond the fire there's a door,

here's a dollar.
There is no dollar

if beyond the fire there's a door
but it only leads to more fire.

"Fuck you." Just aim.
I like a liar. I know your tricks.

"What difference does it make?"
I forbid you to wipe yourself away.

War Story
—a retelling of a Romanian folktale

It's the beginning of things, and the first beast of the air that God creates is the bee. The Gypsy snatches the bee from God's hand, greedy for honey and promising to make votive candles from the wax. God scowls but says nothing. The Gypsy runs home. Then God makes the wasp and gives it to the Romanian, saying, "The Gypsy took the honeybee, so you get this one. Sorry." God winks. The Romanian understands and takes the wasp.

A few days later, he runs into the Gypsy, and they compare notes on their bees.

"Barrels of honey," says the Romanian. "Cisterns brimming with honey. My bee's a beast. Yours?"

The Gypsy pouts. "God tricked me. I've got spoonfuls. Dear Romanian, let's swap!"

"What else can you throw in?"

"My grandfather's Mauser C96! He took it from a dead Nazi!"

"With ammo?"

"With ammo!"

"Deal. My bees are over in that rotten tree."

The Gypsy puts a bowl at the tree's base then swings his ax at the trunk. The wasps, finally freed, attack the Gypsy and sting him until he's blind and paralyzed and they can lay their eggs in him. Wheezing, the Gypsy prays: "Wasp, God tricked me, only you can get back at that fucking Romanian."

Time passes. God forgets. The larvae grow.

The Romanian comes back, sees the Gypsy swollen on the ground, his ax still stuck in the tree. Sucking traces of honey from his moustache, he thinks, "He's lying there like a balloon. I should pop him." He raises the Mauser to his shoulder, fires a round, and wasps, exploding from the corpse that fed them, attack the Romanian and sting him until he's blind and paralyzed and they can lay their eggs in him.

You Have No Idea How Bad It Was

Hard times: if we could eat we believed
Who knew why the war started
When our next meal would come
Life: a grime-stuck bowl on the pantry's highest shelf

Even my tree died my tree
Sprouted from the rubble of my mother's apartment building
Leaves shiny and thick-veined
ROOT OUT INVADERS, the king told us on TV
but I thought *what if it gives me fruit*

A week and the little sapling reached my knees
Two months husband-tall
Its leaves sprang thorns at their tips
They grazed my cheeks when I tended it
I dug out bricks and built a low wall

KILL STRANGERS, blared the king's voice all night
From army trucks roaming the capitol
I stuffed strips from my shirt in my ears
BURN IMAGES THAT ARE NOT MINE
EAT BOOKS AND SHIT OUT THEIR LIES

One morning white blooms covered it
Reeking of gasoline
I danced in mother-rubble
Clapped and sang praises to my tree
Passed out in its shade

I woke
Blooms gone
Black sap oozing
From its wrinkled trunk

Now my enemies have locked me in a cell
And my feet have forgotten my legs
And my lips hate my mouth
And sometimes my fingers crawl up the wall
To the window grate—so hungry
They could eat up all the light

Mirror

I've just buckled my seatbelt when I see a wasp
slip behind the glass
of the passenger side mirror—she doesn't fly out

and I almost bang on the door to scare her off
but change my mind:
she chose this car. Driving to the grocery,

I remember sitting on my neighbor's floor,
taking Valium and watching
planes fly into towers, hearing reports of passengers

who called home, then crashed their hijacked plane
in Pennsylvania. Pushing
my cart through the welcoming *whoosh*

of automatic doors, I admire the neat piles
of Creole tomatoes,
scoop fresh shrimp into a plastic sack.

Bags set in the hatchback, I let the AC run,
sip my Coke. Is she waiting
to get inside and nest under my seat?

Home, putting up the groceries, I imagine ramming
the service cart into the cockpit door,
everyone knowing: *we are going to die together.*

I peel the shrimp and wash my hands.
I carry a can
of prallethrin spray outside and shoot

in the gap between the mirror and its housing.
Nothing flies out.
Sky's clear, wiped clean. Anything might fall.

Toilet Paper

I go down to the basement
to grab a roll of toilet paper from the shelf
but there isn't any

and where the shelf had stood, the wall
is wide open. Inside,
a uniformed man sits at a desk, lamplit,

its top littered with paper—regular paper,
the kind you write on.
There's a chair. The man gestures toward it

so I obey and sit.
The man shuffles some papers, chooses one
and hands it to me, asking

Did you write this?
Being a writer, I'm curious to know
if this is, in fact, my work,

so I take it and try to read it, but the words
tell bloody fantasies
of regicide, slaughter, revenge—I hand it back.

*No, I could never write that. Besides, we have
a president, not a king.*
The man points at the page. I lean in to see

my name, my signature.
The man slides the sheet in a folder, closes it.
What were you looking for

when you came down here? I squirm,
clench my anus shut.
It's personal. His cheap deodorant reeks,

mingles with the basement's mildew, I'm nauseous.
Do you have—what's it called?—
a warrant? The man sighs, removes his glasses,

rubs his eyes. *I didn't come*
to take anything or arrest you. I came to ask
if you know your name

is on all of these. He gestures across the desk.
Behind me, the wall closes.
I hear someone walk down the basement stairs,

hear the plastic crackle
as someone takes a roll from the package
and walks back upstairs

to have, I'm sure, a normal hygienic shit
while I'm stuck reading,
ashamed of my filth, while the man watches.

Ecophobia
1. fear of home.
2. a feeling of powerlessness in the face of cataclysmic change.

I kept a plant. It was—I don't know—
it had leaves? A string
of green hearts—a vine? an ivy?

Every day when I left for work,
I'd worry: what if
I'd overwatered and when I came home,

its roots would've rotted? It got sunlight
all morning, but maybe
that was bad? I've heard sunscreen saves you

from cancer. Do plants get cancer?
Mother brought the plant
when I was sick, said I needed something

to take care of, something that needed me.
One Sunday, hungover,
I found a leaf curled up, brown, fallen

on the windowsill, its siblings poxed.
I backed away. *Asshole*,
I hissed. What if Mother popped by?

She'd say this was my fault, without saying it,
the way they do. Fuck!
Fuck plants! Fuck Mother! When she found me,

I was in the garage, lighter fluid in one hand,
the plant in its pot
burning on the floor, my arm a blazing log.

It's lonely, getting lost in the ridges and valleys
of my scars. Maybe a pet?
A puppy? A parakeet? No, says Mother. No.

The Baker

Lately, I've been baking people
I mold from spit and clay.
Maybe they don't look like people—

headless hat stands? baguettes on tripods?—
but I know what they are
and so do they. At dawn, after they've cooled

on the rack, I set them on a chess board
made from a butcher block.
Each waits, meditating on its shadow, poised

on a light or dark square. Toward noon,
they start to move, wary
of one another as they inch across the board.

Mid-afternoon, something about the light
agitates their limbs,
and they glide, zigzag and tumble

like soldiers dodging bullets. Some cower
in corners, while the rest
collide and merge: a new beast: horn-crowned,

stout, thick-legged, he hunts the others,
his touch poison, paralyzing—
rigid, each sinks into a light or dark square.

The last one caught, the King sinks with it,
the board is empty
and it's dark. So I shut up the shop

and go to bed, and try, under my quilt,
to remember who I am,
panicked until it comes to me:

I am King.

The Palace Astonomer Explicates the New Sky

When they told me you'd called, Your Highness,
to report a missing G-type main-sequence star—
the same yellow dwarf, you said, that stole the sky

each morning of your childhood, shrinking the dark
to your shadow—I smiled and hurried here to see.
Of course you had no telescope: nothing escapes

the royal eye! No twitch in a sniper's sight,
no flicker in a cosmic cloud. Let me confirm,
then, what was to be a birthday surprise:

in your name and image, we're blotting out
each plasma sphere and shiny planet, any dim spark
that might lure our gaze from you. Come to the window,

but not too close. That depthless dark? Your portrait:
no dawn, no dusk, forever. Some specks resist,
flaring back up no matter how we snuff them,

but we're wearing them out. Like the rebels.
Like the professors. Like every traitor
we must protect you from. Good citizens

praise the improved darkness, although
some struggle to adapt—a worker, say,
groping her way home, meets groping hands

or a bayonet. Or some child risks his neck,
head hung back for hours as he stares up
at nothing, trying to track the old stories

he'll soon forget, as your new constitution
helped us forget the old, unruly laws, each
rewritten to make us true to you. So, *star*,

word worse than useless, your enemy, is now
stark in the patriot's lexicon. You need words
that fight for you. *Illuminate?* See: *Eliminate.*

Tonight, your highness, when you thumb
your TV off, after watching your birthday
on the news, and your anthem plays on inside you

my head controls
my head controls
my head controls you all

let your head slump back on the pillow
and behind shut eyes let no tracers sear
the heavens above your capitol.

IV

Larval Psalm

Whatever
the embodied thing
centers its mind on

entirely (the larva,
confined by the wasp
in a hole in the wall,

contemplating
the wasp; the wasp
contemplating

the hole in the wall)
that very form
it attains

without discarding
its former
body.

Testament of the Blue Wasp

The king's voice wobbles across the palace square
        from loudspeakers tucked under gun turret eaves
     slips through brickwork   pavement   sand   to my nest

       some prayer   some rumor of war   some lie   taped
        it's all taped   I've heard it all

      hunched   I sift his words   sorting them
    into heaps of darker   and lighter grains
       some so slick from wind I imagine   wet
         almost remember   water

Listen: I've lived all my lives   here beneath your palace square
     tending my nest   my babies   my babies' ghosts
   before there was a palace   a king   before there was sand
      there was good mud to dig nests in
  cool havens beneath the heat   and my prey understood me

    spider and beetle praised   the mother's kiss
  because I could promise them   *no death through me*
   no death through the mother   *be my babies' meat*

And then your armies came   and donkeys bearing kings
   whining for palaces   of baked brick   and your drills
bored down into my nest   drove me deeper   and drilled past me
  down into stone   for black juice you sucked   and burned

Listen: beetle and spider shriveled   withered in greasy smoke
   and all the kings' carts trucks tanks drills   killed the mud
    left me smoke   to feed my babies   smoke and prayers

     no longer   mother   I am every conjugation
  of death   a memory   buried alive   listening
    to history's hiss   sand slipping   down hollow fistulas
     where I wait   rearranging my nest   my palace

King or ghost of kings: pray   I promise your prayers   will guide me to you
     and the stiff rhythm of my wings   will be breath to you
my legs' ancient hairs   soft to your coarse skin   as smoke to sand

              yield   your voice to mine
    rest in my palace   freed   as mate and meat to me
        let me give you   babies of gold and lapis
              my army   rising

The King in His Chambers, Dying, Alone

Think sand wasp burrowing years under palace undoing grain by
    grain my kingdom
Think sleepless years listening to grain after grain she flicks out from
    under me
Think sand grains rubbed by her leg hairs lightly like fingers on
    glass-rims singing
Think thousands of her hairs lightly billions of grains a swarm singing
Think years sleepless for nightlong droning underground her song for me

Think her swarm-song swelling making room underground for her
Think soldiers stung in alleys dragged home alive like drugged lovers
Think soldiers' numbed flesh soldiers' eyes open to burrow-dark
Think sand wasp straddling soldier's belly her eyes dark moons above
Think sand wasp's egg-spike piercing his soft belly

Think eggs snug in meat-warmth swelling first hungers growing
Think hatched grubs eating blind making room for more hunger
Think soldiers round as mothers duty done deaf to swarm-song
Think wasp queen's armies bursting free
Think drones done with meat-life burrowing more burrow its ceiling
    sky now where their queen flies free

Think a sand wasp crowned on my throne
and flags' shadows scudding down vacant halls
and flags' shadows scudding down vacant halls
and nightlong sleepless underground I'll drone

Winged Fictory

She used to stand right there, atop a tall calumny
in the palace square.
A sloppy sort of sundial, with those flowing folds,

those thick-spread wings. And on top of that,
she'd been beheaded!
By the King, some said, though no one knew,

dared ask why. Kids picked fallen plumage
from the cobblestones,
sharpened shafts to prick tattoos

on cowards' faces. Inscribed on the granite base,
her motto: WE WIN WARS,
repeated, all the way around. Her head

was said to be bedded in an eagle's nest
or babbling in a brook
or book, or rotting in a bucket in a shed,

the way things do when kids forget. "WE WIN WARS!"
we scouts shouted
as we marched around the square on Fictory Day,

WE WIN WARS blazoned on our caps, little fists blistered
from snatching at wasps
that swarmed our sweaty corporeality. Then your armies came

and poof, all her feathers fell, her robes flapped away,
gone. Bombs
cratered this and that, toppled our acanthine columns.

Still the calumny stands. Its shadows
tell the hours. That's
the way it is, I guess, with powers.

Palace Inventory

I prefer not to know too much
about my clients. My reputation attracts them
as the need arises. They have things they need sorted
and enumerated and catalogued. These things
are always a mess. Really, a fucking mess. Sensitive
messes, sensitive needs. They need my uncommon sense
not to need to understand the meaning
of the mess. Just its shape, which is the shape
its parts make. If I knew more than that,
I might as well be them.

This time, it was a palace. Got on a plane in one city,
slept, landed in another city you've probably heard of
on the news, but what's the news? Sloppy inventories.
Sloppy inventories of other people's pain
whose meaning means nothing. That's a fact. If you knew
what I know, you wouldn't want to know
how meaningless it all is. Causes. Effects. Pain
is not part of the inventory. Pain
is an epiphenomenon of facts.

We land. A jeep whisks me through dust
that stinks of burnt oil and bodies. Some human, some not.
Bodies on the roadside, civilians, soldiers, bodies we swerve
to keep going. Bodies exploded, bellies cratered
as if they'd swallowed small bombs.
But they weren't what I was there for.

Our jeep stalls on the way.
The driver gets out to look under the hood.
A dead soldier lies in the ditch beside us.
It's hot. I can smell him. A wasp descends,
hovers, lands on his lip. Another. Dozens, hundreds.
By the time the driver slams the hood shut and starts the engine,
the soldier's face is a humming mask.

We arrive at the palace square.
Some soldiers are watching old women
and children, some missing arms or legs,
as they make piles of clothes, broken furniture, cartons
spilling folders and photographs and spools of audio tape.
These piles were burning. The smoke weighed down the light.

The palace was empty.
It could have been any vacant building.
Colorless rooms awaiting orders.
Every empty inch. Every shadow of an inch.

Burrow Inventory

1.
The absence of *wasp*   is _____.
The absence of *burrow*   is _____.

Grub   is the *ghost*   of *egg*.
Husk   is the *ghost*   of *host*.
Wasp   is the *ghost*   of *grub*.

Thought   is a *burrow* for *flight*.
Flight   is the *end* of *thought*.

2.
Her scent smeared on these walls
These walls scraped by her claws
Her claws tracing battles in air—

Drawn by her scent, ant-like, I crawl in
seeking refuge from death, lower
my head, pray *destroy my enemies*.

3.
Palace razed, palatial gravel fills
her burrow. Lone and level,
gravel grinds down to sand.

At a rubble field's edge, a wasp clutches
a stung beetle. Eggs hungering, her claws flick
grit to air, dusting her wings as she digs—

How I Will Remember Paradise

Watching a wasp drowse on a windfall quince;
chalk dust on my last roses.

Across the road, where army bulldozers
have razed the bombed-out school,

soldiers unload lumber and stack pallets of bricks
for the new school they're building.

Blackberry vines have trained themselves
around the rebar left from the garden wall.

One soldier, stripped to the waist, strides smiling
through the gate and asks for a drink of water.

I hand him the hose, twist the spigot, watch his lips
as he sucks at the feeble stream, douses his hair,

lets the water rinse his thin dirty chest.
He turns off the tap, loops the hose on its hook,

asks me *Is that rosemary?* Yes, I tell him.
His pants barely hang on his hips. Why

is he still standing here? *You must be glad
about the school*, he says. One day, I tell him,

a teacher, crossing the street after lunch,
twitched, kneeled,

and collapsed: a sniper's target practice.
And then round after round of shells

blasted the school and half the houses.
When I could finally walk outside again,

pale dust whitened every leaf and stem.
No water to rinse them. They stood

for weeks like that, like statues. He smiles.
That sounds beautiful. Yes, I tell him. Maybe

when it's safe, you'll help me clear the rubble
from my garden wall. Maybe we'll find

a little body, berries crushed in its fists—
I step closer—beautiful, everything—

he thanks me for the water.

After the Last War

For years, I left the TV on all night
so I could fall asleep to the royal anthem
turned low, playing until dawn, white noise

to stifle my dreams: enemy hands
lifting me alive from rubble, caressing
my face, over my mouth, smothering me.

Then war came: shelling, screams, sirens.
The power went out a lot. Eyes shut,
day and night, I lay in bed and sang.

War ended, and the power stays on
most nights. I watch TV before bed.
The new anthem plays. A loud presenter

narrates in new words the footage
they keep looping: the king's riddled body
in the palace square, enemy soldiers

marching royal guards, their hands raised
as if warding off the wasp swarms
droning over the city. I turn it off,

humming a dead man's birthday song.

Economy

All I wanted
was a cup
of water,
just a sip
to keep me
long enough
to tell how
even a cup
in still life
or lip-tilted
video flicker,
cracked, empty,
could flood
the dust-clouded
farms and
highways and
townships' shuttered
strip malls,
how, banked
with grasses
and trees'
cool shade,
my dreams
would flow free
and I'd ride
on a raft
to the sea.

Homecoming

1.
Finally the war was over
and we could go home but
my wife was wary. *Those houses?*

she said, watching the news.
Those stores? schools? police? Fake.
Don't believe what you see.

Childhood. Wasps twitching on honey cakes,
and our game with the clay balls, hiding them
under the house—what was it called?

I phoned my brother. He couldn't
remember. He wasn't going back.
You hear "it's hell, they're starving,"

then, "such progress, it's amazing."
Who cares anymore. Let me be
unhappy where I am.

A neighbor who'd helped us
when we immigrated flew back
to check on family property.

Weeks later, I saw her
in the shade on her porch,
drinking tea.   *How was it?*

How long should we wait?
Her skin had darkened. Not tanned,
more like it came from inside her.

Wait a year. Five. Ten. By then, who knows—
maybe everywhere will be like that.

2.
Everything looked too new. Ruins
all razed and dumped, the palace
a musuem and shops, the square

a civic theater. The supermarket
was like a supermarket, but the food
tasted like imitations of food we knew.

The library gates were locked.
Under renovation. Opening soon.

Of course our old house was gone.
Our new one was fine. Familiar,
like the groceries. The power

went out or we had no water
for hours, sometimes all day.
It's just how things are here,

said our new neighbors. We tried
making friends, but their chatter
and ours sounded like a script.

We watched a lot of TV.
Scientists urged us to be vigilant
about eradicating invasive species.

3.
*Call your brother and ask him
to send some real toothpaste.*

My wife spat in the sink, cupped
her hand under the faucet,
caught the thin, cloudy stream.

My brother didn't answer.
No message. Toothpaste—
I just couldn't say it.

That night, at the civic theater,
we saw a folk play. No story,
just symbols—an iron eagle

with a red tongue, iron bars
for feathers, wingtips curled
into blunt iron fists—and phrases

sung by a children's chorus.
Wings of peace, bird of hope . . .

When we came home, the street
was dark. My wife found her flashlight
and led the way.
                  Oh my god, she said,

look. The beam lit a heap of dark husks
in a mound on the seat of my reading chair.
Wasps, I said. *They must have nested*

in the walls. I wonder what killed them.
My wife was grabbing garbage bags
and handed me the broom: more mounds

on the dining table, in the laundry basket,
on the bathroom scale, in our bed.
She held the flashlight, I swept the bodies.

In the morning, bags were heaped
in front of every house on the block.

4.
Now the power and water have stopped
for good. We left coffee cans in the yard,
hoping to catch rain. One day, packs

of batteries and cases of bottled water
showed up. My wife twisted off a cap,
sipped. *Fake. Even the water.*

At night, people come out
to scavenge. We hear them
rustling in our garden.

Days, my wife shuts the door
to her room, stays there reading
the same books she brought with her,

while I've been working
in the basement, ever since I dropped
a wrench on the concrete floor

and heard under the clang a muffled
echo. I took a mallet, tapped lightly,
heard it again, a buried breath. I heaved

the mallet, cracked the slab, pried
chunks away and found the burrow
someone had started, the shovel

they'd left. It feels good, digging, aiming
into the dark, feeling it resist, breaking it
down, shoulders sore, back sore, it feels

like it means something, this rhythm
of blade into dirt calling
come home   come home

you're almost there

Notes
Compiled by Dr. E.A. Melville

"How the Torturers Come to Truth"—My efforts at piecing together the tunnel-world have been frustrated by not having access to, among other things, its codes of justice, the outcomes of which are consistent only in their prolix cruelty. In this text, as in others, it is unclear whether the actions described are factual or fantasy, or whether those describing them discern a difference. A related but fragmentary and confused account (not included in this volume) describes an army liberating a country from a despot, yet, rather than releasing his political prisoners, actually arresting more citizens the liberators themselves deem suspect, and torturing them. I am reminded of certain insects who colonize other insects' nests and eat their young.

"Waspocrypha"—How fortunate we are to live in an age in which what was once called mental illness has been eradicated! And yet is impossible to navigate this text without sharing its author-compiler's lucid mania, the nature of which I cannot peg more precisely than as a species of religious fervor. This is, I confess, my favorite item in the bundle, the one I return to most often for pure literary pleasure, not only because it includes so much poetry from this civilization (assuming any of these sources are real) but because the compiler and the clerk believe some mystery will be revealed through what are only chance associations among texts that consider, however incidentally, monstrous wasps. I feel a kinship. I almost understand. I believe, at times, that if it had been me, I would have known exactly what requests to tender to that late assistant file clerk.

"Asylum"—I take this narrative to have had one of two purposes. On the one hand, it may be the literal account of one woman's tragically thwarted attempt to find some measure of freedom and safety, based on her diary and items retrieved from investigators' files in her home kingdom and the country to which she attempted to immigrate. In that case, it may have been intended to expose the cruelty and injustice of both regimes, and the Editor may well have risked his life in compiling and publishing it.

On the other hand, the narrative may be a spiritual allegory, the poetic fragments the remnants of ancient sources, and the Editor a religious scholar whose duty was to keep these teaching stories alive for each age. This would be evidence of a profoundly devout tradition with a complex and, for us, inscrutable relationship to the wasp cult. In this case, it may even be possible that the narrators of "Surveillance Notes" are not, as they appear to be, threatening figures with designs on the poet's life, but pilgrims who have come to seek out her wisdom.

In either case, this woman's journey is a microcosm of the tunnel-bundle as a whole.

"the Geographical Encyclopedia"—Another source that I have wished I could consult. At times, I have even imagined that I might find our country there.

"Editor."—Another source that I have wished I could consult. Another kinship.

"Homecoming"—This text brings to mind the words of the orphaned prophet: "And I only am escaped alone to tell thee."

Thanks

Many hands, eyes, and generous minds made this book possible. The following people contributed in one way or another to the genesis and ultimate form of *Parasite Kingdom*:

Alice Notley, whose workshop comments on an early draft from this project (one that didn't survive as a poem, but in which I was tentatively exploring this material) gave me the permission I needed to create and inhabit this kingdom.

Bryan Borland and Seth Pennington, of Sibling Rivalry Press, whose encouraging comments on an early chapbook version of this project also kept me going.

Kelly Anne Mueller, whose artwork gives me much joy and inspiration.

Susan Bernofsky, Tonya M. Foster, Elizabeth Gross, Dana Sonnenschein: thank you for long friendship and the many ways, subtle and overt, that you helped.

My workshop group, in its shifting constellations over the years this project took: Katy Balma, Allison Campbell, Peter Cooley, Melissa Dickey, Carolyn Hembree, Rodney Jones, Laura Mullen, Kay Murphy, Ed Skoog, Andy Stallings, Andrea Young. I am grateful to each of you.

My students at Lusher Charter School, especially my upper-level certificate of artistry creative writing class in 2017-2018, who critiqued various drafts of the poem that became "Economy": I am grateful for what I learned from you.

Leslie McGrath, who selected this manuscript for the Tenth Gate Prize: thank you for your enthusiasm, encouragement, rigor, and patience. I could not have asked for a better reader.

Nancy White, publisher of The Word Works: thank you, again.

Thank you to the *New York Times* photographers who took the photographs in Eastern Ghouta, Syria, which were the basis for "Four Photographs of a Man Carrying a Child." (This thank-you feels woefully inadequate, as I can only imagine the conditions under which those photographs were taken.)

Finally, a note to George W. Bush, Donald Rumsfeld, John Yoo, John Ashcroft, the American torturers at Abu Ghraib, Barack Obama (reluctantly), Donald Trump, Stephen Bannon, Stephen Miller, et al.: I am not grateful to you, but without you, I would not have known the anger and despair that drove me to finish this book. I dedicate it to your victims, past, present, and future.

About the Author

Brad Richard's previous books include *Habitations* (Portal Press 2000); *Motion Studies*, winner of the Washington Prize and finalist for the 2012 Thom Gunn Award in Gay Poetry from the Publishing Triangle; and *Butcher's Sugar* (Sibling Rivalry Press, 2012). He has also published two chapbooks, *The Men in the Dark* (Lowlands Press, 2004) and *Curtain Optional* (Press Street, 2011). His poems and reviews have appeared in journals such as *American Letters & Commentary*, *The Iowa Review*, *Massachusetts Review*, *Mississippi Review*, *Prairie Schooner*, and many others.

Richard lives in New Orleans where he directs the creative writing program at Lusher Charter High School. He also co-directs the Scholastic Art & Writing Awards of Southeast Louisiana, a regional affiliate of the Alliance for Young Artists & Writers, and co-curates The Waves, a LGBTQ+ reading series.

He was the 2015 Louisiana Artist of the Year and recipient of awards and fellowships from Poets & Writers, Inc., The Surdna Foundation, the National Endowment for the Humanities, and the Louisiana Division of the Arts. For more information please go to bradrichard.org.

About the Artist

Originally from Chicago, Kelly moved to Jackson, MS, after receiving her MFA at Northern Illinois University, and on to Baton Rouge, LA, only two weeks before Katrina. She is currently a member of both The Front Gallery in New Orleans and the Baton Rouge Gallery, and has exhibited with New Context/Kasia Kay Gallery in Chicago and in the Scope art fair in Miami and New York. Her work has been published in *New American Paintings* and *Studio Visit Magazine*. An art teacher at Lusher Charter School, her many residencies include a Surdna Fellowship in Brazil's Amazon Rainforest.

About The Word Works

Since its founding in 1974, The Word Works has published volumes of contemporary poetry and presented public programs. Its imprints include The Washington Prize, The Tenth Gate Prize, The Hilary Tham Capital Collection, and International Editions.

Monthly, The Word Works offers free literary programs in the Café Muse reading series at the Writers Center of Bethesda, MD, and each summer it holds free poetry programs in Washington, D.C.'s Rock Creek Park. Word Works programs have included "In the Shadow of the Capitol," a symposium and archival project on the African American intellectual community in segregated Washington, D.C.; the Gunston Arts Center Poetry Series; the Poet Editor panel discussions at The Writer's Center; Master Class workshops; and a writing retreat in Tuscany, Italy.

As a 501(c)3 organization, The Word Works has received awards from the National Endowment for the Arts, the National Endowment for the Humanities, the D.C. Commission on the Arts & Humanities, the Witter Bynner Foundation, Poets & Writers, The Writer's Center, Bell Atlantic, the David G. Taft Foundation, and others, including many generous private patrons.

An archive of artistic and administrative materials in the Washington Writing Archive housed in the George Washington University Gelman Library. It is a member of the Community of Literary Magazines and Presses and its books are distributed by Small Press Distribution.

wordworksbooks.org

OTHER WORD WORKS BOOKS

Annik Adey-Babinski, *Okay Cool No Smoking Love Pony*
Karren L. Alenier, *Wandering on the Outside*
Karren L. Alenier, ed., *Whose Woods These Are*
Karren L. Alenier & Miles David Moore, eds.,
　　Winners: A Retrospective of the Washington Prize
Christopher Bursk, ed., *Cool Fire*
Willa Carroll, *Nerve Chorus*
Grace Cavalieri, *Creature Comforts*
Abby Chew, *A Bear Approaches from the Sky*
Nadia Colburn, *The High Shelf*
Barbara Goldberg, *Berta Broadfoot and Pepin the Short*
Akua Lezli Hope, *Them Gone*
Frannie Lindsay, *If Mercy*
Elaine Magarrell, *The Madness of Chefs*
Marilyn McCabe, *Glass Factory*
Kevin McLellan, *Ornitheology*
JoAnne McFarland, *Identifying the Body*
Leslie McGrath, *Feminists Are Passing from Our Lives*
Ann Pelletier, *Letter That Never*
Ayaz Pirani, *Happy You Are Here*
W.T. Pfefferle, *My Coolest Shirt*
Jacklyn Potter, Dwaine Rieves, Gary Stein, eds.,
　　Cabin Fever: Poets at Joaquin Miller's Cabin
Robert Sargent, *Aspects of a Southern Story*
　　& A Woman from Memphis
Miles Waggener, *Superstition Freeway*
Fritz Ward, *Tsunami Diorama*
Camille-Yvette Welsch, *The Four Ugliest Children in Christendom*
Amber West, *Hen & God*
Maceo Whitaker, *Narco Farm*
Nancy White, ed., *Word for Word*

THE TENTH GATE PRIZE

Jennifer Barber, *Works on Paper*, 2015
Lisa Lewis, *Taxonomy of the Missing*, 2017
Brad Richard, *Parasite Kingdom*, 2018
Roger Sedarat, *Haji As Puppet*, 2016
Lisa Sewell, *Impossible Object*, 2014

INTERNATIONAL EDITIONS

Kajal Ahmad (Alana Marie Levinson-LaBrosse, Mewan Nahro Said Sofi, and Darya Abdul-Karim Ali Najin, trans., with Barbara Goldberg), *Handful of Salt*
Keyne Cheshire (trans.), *Murder at Jagged Rock: A Tragedy by Sophocles*
Jeannette L. Clariond (Curtis Bauer, trans.), *Image of Absence*
Jean Cocteau (Mary-Sherman Willis, trans.), *Grace Notes*
Yoko Danno & James C. Hopkins, *The Blue Door*
Moshe Dor, Barbara Goldberg, Giora Leshem, eds., *The Stones Remember: Native Israeli Poets*
Moshe Dor (Barbara Goldberg, trans.), *Scorched by the Sun*
Laura Cesarco Eglin (Jesse Lee Kercheval and Catherine Jagoe, trans.), *Reborn in Ink*
Vladimir Levchev (Henry Taylor, trans.), *Black Book of the Endangered Species*

THE WASHINGTON PRIZE

Nathalie Anderson, *Following Fred Astaire*, 1998
Michael Atkinson, *One Hundred Children Waiting for a Train*, 2001
Molly Bashaw, *The Whole Field Still Moving Inside It*, 2013
Carrie Bennett, *biography of water*, 2004
Peter Blair, *Last Heat*, 1999
John Bradley, *Love-in-Idleness: The Poetry of Roberto Zingarello*, 1995, 2ND
    edition 2014
Christopher Bursk, *The Way Water Rubs Stone*, 1988
Richard Carr, *Ace*, 2008
Jamison Crabtree, *Rel[AM]ent*, 2014
Jessica Cuello, *Hunt*, 2016
Barbara Duffey, *Simple Machines*, 2015
B. K. Fischer, *St. Rage's Vault*, 2012
Linda Lee Harper, *Toward Desire*, 1995
Ann Rae Jonas, *A Diamond Is Hard But Not Tough*, 1997
Susan Lewis, *Zoom*, 2017
Frannie Lindsay, *Mayweed*, 2009
Richard Lyons, *Fleur Carnivore*, 2005
Elaine Magarrell, *Blameless Lives*, 1991
Fred Marchant, *Tipping Point*, 1993, 2ND edition 2013
Nils Michals, *Gembox*
Ron Mohring, *Survivable World*, 2003
Barbara Moore, *Farewell to the Body*, 1990
Brad Richard, *Motion Studies*, 2010
Jay Rogoff, *The Cutoff*, 1994
Prartho Sereno, *Call from Paris*, 2007, 2ND edition 2013
Enid Shomer, *Stalking the Florida Panther*, 1987
John Surowiecki, *The Hat City After Men Stopped Wearing Hats*, 2006
Miles Waggener, *Phoenix Suites*, 2002
Charlotte Warren, *Gandhi's Lap*, 2000
Mike White, *How to Make a Bird with Two Hands*, 2011
Nancy White, *Sun, Moon, Salt*, 1992, 2ND edition 2010
George Young, *Spinoza's Mouse*, 1996

THE HILARY THAM CAPITAL COLLECTION

Nathalie Anderson, *Stain*
Mel Belin, *Flesh That Was Chrysalis*
Carrie Bennett, *The Land Is a Painted Thing*
Doris Brody, *Judging the Distance*
Sarah Browning, *Whiskey in the Garden of Eden*
Grace Cavalieri, *Pinecrest Rest Haven*
Cheryl Clarke, *By My Precise Haircut*
Christopher Conlon, *Gilbert and Garbo in Love*
  & *Mary Falls: Requiem for Mrs. Surratt*
Donna Denizé, *Broken Like Job*
W. Perry Epes, *Nothing Happened*
David Eye, *Seed*
Bernadette Geyer, *The Scabbard of Her Throat*
Elizabeth Gross, *this body / that lightning show*
Barbara G. S. Hagerty, *Twinzilla*
Lisa Hase-Jackson, *Flint & Fire*
James Hopkins, *Eight Pale Women*
Donald Illich, *Chance Bodies*
Brandon Johnson, *Love's Skin*
Thomas March, *Aftermath*
Marilyn McCabe, *Perpetual Motion*
Judith McCombs, *The Habit of Fire*
James McEwen, *Snake Country*
Miles David Moore, *The Bears of Paris* & *Rollercoaster*
Kathi Morrison-Taylor, *By the Nest*
Tera Vale Ragan, *Reading the Ground*
Michael Shaffner, *The Good Opinion of Squirrels*
Maria Terrone, *The Bodies We Were Loaned*
Hilary Tham, *Bad Names for Women* & *Counting*
Barbara Ungar, *Charlotte Brontë, You Ruined My Life* & *Immortal Medusa*
Jonathan Vaile, *Blue Cowboy*
Rosemary Winslow, *Green Bodies*
Michele Wolf, *Immersion*
Joe Zealberg, *Covalence*